CARDIFF
THEN *and* NOW

Brian Lee and Russell Harvey

breedon **books**
PUBLISHING

First published in Great Britain in 2001 by
The Breedon Books Publishing Company Limited
Breedon House, 3 The Parker Centre, Derby, DE21 4SZ.

ISBN 1 85983 253 9

Printed and bound by Butler & Tanner, Frome, Somerset
Jacket printing by GreenShires Ltd, Leicester

CARDIFF
THEN *and* NOW

Contents

Introduction 7

City Streets 10

Transport 34

Shops and Businesses 55

Leisure and Pleasure 74

Vanished Docklands 103

Cardiff Bay Today 117

Out and About 123

Acknowledgements

The authors would like to thank the following people for allowing us to use their photographs as without their help this book would never have been compiled. Dennis Pope of Pope's Photo Service, Arthur Weston Evans, Allen Hambly, Emily Donovan, Ruby Howe, Harvey Bennett, John Meazey and David Davies, FRICS of Stephenson & Alexander, Auctioners, High Street, Cardiff.

Thanks are also due to the editors of the *Western Mail, South Wales Echo* and *Cardiff Post* for publishing our requests to their readers for the loan of their photographs and to the staff of the Local Studies Department Cardiff County Council for their help over the years.

Introduction

The Welsh capital has been well documented in the past with an excellent choice of picture books appertaining to this cosmopolitan city, Stewart Williams's *Cardiff Yesterday* series of 36 volumes being just one example.

However, of all the books that have been compiled about this vibrant city *Cardiff: Then and Now* is the ultimate walk down Memory Lane. For the first time ever, old images of street scenes and buildings – some dating back a hundred years and others much more recent – are pictured on the same page as modern-day pictures allowing the reader to compare the old town with the new one which was made a city in 1905 and named the official capital of Wales in 1955.

The exception is the chapter on the docklands which have been transformed beyond all recognition. Still, the section of photographs showing dockers at work will give readers a fascinating insight to this once important port.

The captions to the photographs are both interesting and informative. For instance, how many Cardiffians know that Queen Street was once known as Crockherbtown until it was renamed in honour of Queen Victoria in 1886? Or did you know that Cardiff once boasted that it had 'The World's Greatest Bazaar' as well as 'The Cheapest Clothiers in the World'?

Or that in Womanby Street in 1759 a fight took place between sailors armed with pistols, swords, pikes and muskets? Cardiff's famous castle, the city's oldest building, has witnessed nearly 2,000 years of history and it is no surprise that being in the heart of Cardiff it features on more than one page.

And while it has changed very little (from the outside at least) since the first postcards of it were published around 100 years ago, it is interesting to note when studying the ensuing pages the changes that have taken place directly around it with regard to the different modes of transport and the clothes which people wore.

Cardiff has always been a city of change and Matthew Williams, curator of Cardiff Castle, claims that as early as the 1860s, residents of the town were commenting sadly on the rapid changes that were taking place. Some of these changes have been for the good but not all of them.

The inexcusable filling in of the old Glamorgan Canal in 1945 and the demolishing of Herbert House, the ancient site of Greyfriars in 1958, are just two examples of acts of vandalism by the then city fathers. This unique book charts many of the changes that have taken place in Cardiff over the years and should appeal to both the young and the old. And as Matthew Williams says, 'Nothing evokes nostalgia quite like an old photograph. Suddenly the past comes alive before our eyes as we once again look at long-forgotten faces and places.' How much more so then when we have an up-to-date picture to compare it with the old one.

'I have pleasant
memories of days spent
in Cardiff, when with
more useful steps I trod
its streets, and wandered
in its pleasant by-ways.'

*John Kyrle Fletcher (Cardiff Notes
Picturesque and Biographical) 1920*

Opposite: City Hall, Cardiff. The foundation stone of the City Hall was laid by the Marquess of Bute on 23 October 1901.

City Streets

Once the main street of the medieval borough, annual fairs were held in High Street in front of the guildhall. The first guildhall was built in 1331. The last guildhall, built in 1767, was demolished in 1860. The tram lines tell us that this picture was taken around 1902 the year trams came to Cardiff.

Only the historic Cardiff Castle centre of picture remains the same.

World War One was in its second year when this postcard of Queen Street was posted in 1915. Once known as Crockherbtown, Queen Street was renamed in honour of Queen Victoria by resolution of the town council in December 1886. Crockherbtown is believed to have got its name from the fact that crock-herbs or pot herbs were once grown in the area.

The tram lines and ornate street lighting have long disappeared and although the façades of some of the buildings have changed one can still recognise this end of Queen Street.

This smart, young lady with a smile on her pretty face is walking along the Dumfries Place end of Queen Street. The houses seen in the centre of the picture were demolished in 1978 to make way for a multi-storey car park.

The girl in the top photograph would find a vast difference to this part of the city if she could walk down it today.

Top Shop on the corner of Windsor Place and Queen Street, like Austin Reed on the opposite corner, is just a memory. The Capitol cinema was situated on the opposite side of the street, *c.*1970.

Some would suggest that this particular part of the city looked more attractive before it was modernised. The building on the right is now Barclays Bank.

This picture of Queen Street was taken in the 1950s before the city centre streets were pedestrianised in 1958. Evan Roberts Ltd store can be seen left of picture on the corner of Kingsway.

The shop names have changed, but the traffic lights appear to be in exactly the same spot as they were in the top picture.

In this picture of Queen Street, taken after the streets had been pedestrianised, Evan Roberts Ltd is to the right of picture. It is hard to imagine that near this spot Cardiffians in the 1750s gathered to the bullring to watch dogs attack bulls tethered to a wooden post. Even harder to imagine that this 'entertainment' was sponsored by the town council.

The telephone kiosk in this picture is one of the KX 100s launched in the 1990s. The ones in the top picture are two of the K8's launched in 1968.

The statue of John, the second Marquis of Bute, is left of this postcard sent in 1913. The statue was sculptured by I. Evan Thomas and was originally erected in front of the High Street Town Hall in 1853 and moved to St Mary Street in 1879.

The Marquis of Bute's statue is missing from this picture. In 1999 Cardiff Bay Development Corporation submitted plans to relocate the statue to a location in Bute Street. The canal bridge, extreme right of the top picture, was removed in 1952. The Terminus Hotel also seen to the right of top picture was originally known as the Steam Mills.

This rare postcard shows the corner of St Mary Street and Wood Street around 1905. The tobacconist on the corner was popular with generations of children who were fascinated by the large stuffed brown bear in the shop. The bear can still be seen today in a tobacconist shop in Wyndham Arcade.

There may be a few chimney stacks missing from this picture compared to the top one, but the façades of the buildings have changed very little indeed. And, of course, motor cars have taken over from horse-drawn vehicles.

The Royal Hotel, left of picture. The oblong advertisement seen directly above the gentleman's trilby is advertising D'Arc's Waxworks later known as the Continental Waxworks. The waxworks came to Cardiff in 1866 and closed in 1946.

When this picture was taken the Royal Hotel was undergoing a multi-million pound refurbishment.

This outline image of a church on the wall in Great Western Lane is thought to depict St Mary's Church which is thought to have stood near this spot. The principal church of the town, it was destroyed in the great floods of 1607. St Mary Street took its name from the medieval church, *c.*1948.

The car park and the advertisement boards may be long gone but apart from that there is no mistaking Great Western Lane today.

Note the trolley bus wires in this picture of Wood Street. The last trolley bus ran from Wood Street to Llandaff Fields in 1966. The street was named after Colonel Wood who owned land in the area.

Two storeys have been added to St David's House since the top picture was taken. Motorists will certainly notice the double yellow lines too!

The Cardiff Arms Park private car park in Westgate Street during the 1970s. The River Taff once ran along Westgate Street and it was in 1849 that work commenced on diverting the course of the river.

The Millennium Stadium was officially opened by Prime Minister Tony Blair in 1999. The remaining section of wall seen right of both pictures is the clue that the new stadium rose on the site of the old.

Westgate Street entrance to the Glamorgan County Cricket Club at the Cardiff Arms Park. The club was founded in the Angel Hotel in 1888, *c*.1970.

The trees have gone and only a small part of the old wall left of picture remains. The flats, also left of picture, were built in 1939 and have recently been refurbished.

The magnificent house covered in ivy, 20 Park Place, is known as Park House. It was constructed in 1874 by Lord Bute for his engineer Mr McConnochie and was designed by the world renowned Cardiff architect William Burges.

Park House is easily recognisable by its chimney stack.

This former smart dwelling stood at number 13 Park Place but was looking worse for wear when this picture was taken in March 1974. The forecourt of the Norwich Union Insurance building can be seen left of picture. Park Place was formerly known as Dobbinpitts Road and Blind Lane.

Oakleigh House office block now stands on the corner of Park Place and Stuttgarter Strasse.

Charles Street in 1968. It was named after Charles Vachell who was elected Mayor of Cardiff in 1849 and 1855. He played an important part in the implementation of the Public Health Act (1848) in Cardiff, because of his concern over the poor living conditions of Cardiffians. The white building in the distance is Seccombes which was situated in Queen Street and which closed in 1977. St David's Cathedral is extreme left of picture.

The houses have disappeared in this picture as they were demolished to make way for Cathedral Walk.

The gentlemen's toilets in Kingsway. The North Gate of the old town was near this spot.

Apart from the demolition of the gents lavatory in the top picture, very little seems to have changed in between the fifty-odd years these two photographs were taken.

Originally built in the 12th. century as a chapel of ease to St
Mary's, St John's Church is the oldest church in the city centre.
Between 1739-1818 the area below its famous tower, designed
by John Hart, housed the town's fire engine.

Repair work to the steeple of St John's Church was taking place when this picture was taken.

The corner of Newport Road and Fitzalan Road. Behind the motor cars in Newport Road can be seen the old University College of South Wales and Monmouthshire, *c.*1950.

Newport Road has seen many changes since the top picture was taken.

Frederick Street was at one time little more than a country lane and until 1846 the town's cattle market was held in the street. The street was demolished in the 1970s.

It is hard to pinpoint the exact spot, but Raebur House in the top picture was somewhere in the vicinity of this picture.

Larkins Wholesalers, Hills Terrace, during the 1950s. Frederick Street is extreme left of picture and Canal Street right of picture.

Part of the new County Library, which was officially opened in 1988, can be seen left of picture in what is now St David's Link.

Working Street. When this picture was taken in the 1970s, a packet of low tar Embassy extra mild cigarettes as advertised on the advertising board cost 53 pence.

The tree left of picture is clearly the same one as seen in the top picture. St David's Hall officially opened by Queen Elizabeth, the Queen Mother, in 1983 is to the right of tree.

City Transport

Like the vehicle pictured on the right of picture, opposite the Terminus Hotel, the early horse bus and tram services established in Cardiff under the Tramways Act of 1870, were privately owned. But by the late 1890s the run down condition of these vehicles led the corporation to seek Parliamentary powers to take control of them.

The buildings to the left have changed very little in a hundred years. However, the Terminus Hotel is now known as Sam's Bar and boasts a ghost.

To the left of this postcard can be seen the Dick Kerr 52-seat open-top tram introduced to the town on 1 May 1902. To the right, a horse-bus which operated between Cardiff Castle and Conway Road is awaiting passengers, *c.*1909.

Cardiff Castle has witnessed many modes of traffic over the years as these two pictures illustrate.

Horse traps and carriages appeared to be the order of the day when this postcard, sent by a sailor bound for Port Said on the SS *Dart* with a cargo of coal in 1904, was posted.

Horse-drawn carriages no longer drive past Cardiff Castle and no longer does grape vines grow on the castle walls as can be seen in the top picture.

Double deck open-top tram cars, which were housed at purpose built depots at Newport Road and Clare Road, like the one in this scene, had replaced all the horse trams by October 1902. But horse and carriages were still popular when this picture was taken in Queen Street around 1908.

Shank's pony is the only form of transport seen in this picture.

This was Queen Street in 1915 during World War One. Because of the shortage of male staff, conductresses became a familiar sight on trams.

The only mode of transport that can be seen in this photograph is the bicycle the man is wheeling to the right of picture.

Buses and trolley buses transported Cardiffians to and from town when this picture was taken in Queen Street during the 1950s.

Pedestrian crossings, as seen in the top picture, first came into use in Cardiff in 1936.

One of the early single deck trams seen here in Queen Street around 1902.

A new single deck bus picks up a passenger in Greyfriars Road.

Queen Street Bridge. A day return rail ticket to London cost £3.45 when this picture was taken in 1972. To the right can be seen part of the platform of Queen Street Railway Station.

When this picture was taken work had commenced on transforming the AA building – note the scaffolding extreme right – into luxury flats.

Queen Street Railway Station, Station Terrace. It was at one time known as the Taff Vale Railway Station. The Taff Vale Railway was opened in 1840 and ran between Cardiff and Abercynon. The following year the line was extended to Merthyr Tydfil. The Cory Hall and YMCA right of picture were demolished in 1983.

The new Queen Street station is not a patch on the old one which had a lot more character about it. Note the absence of parked cars right of picture.

The railway line that daily takes scores of people to Cardiff Bay from Queen Street Station is shown right of picture. Owing to the height of the railway bridge at the north end of Bute Street, only single deck trolley buses could be used along this route in the 1950s.

The old Salvation Army Hostel has been demolished and the wall right of picture now hides the railway line.

The Central Square Bus Station was opened in 1954 but this picture was taken some time later. The gentleman wearing a trilby doesn't look too happy. Perhaps the bus he is waiting for is late again!

These days passengers are protected from the elements thanks to these glass covered shelters.

Central Square Bus Station. Note the trolley bus wires. Trolley buses replaced trams on the Wood Street and Clarence Road route in 1942. The last trolley bus ran on 11 January 1970 when special tickets were issued. A decorated vehicle ran on the Ely route. The building left of picture is the old Wood Street School used as the Cardiff Corporation Transport Depot. Work on a new purpose-built office block adjacent to the depot commenced in 1970.

With all the building work that has gone on in the area recently, Central Square Bus Station is hardly recognisable now.

Adam Street Bridge was once known as Newtown Bridge. The two gentlemen to the right of picture are standing in front of an advertisement for the Odeon Cinema. The film advertised is *Tarzan and the Jungle Queen* which starred Lex Barker, *c.*1951.

Some things never change. Brains Brewers are still advertising their beers on the bridge. Note the BT building left of picture which has sprung up.

Bute Street Bridge looking from Hayes Bridge Road, *c.*1970.

The bridge which is on the main Cardiff to Swansea line is still in use but all the buildings in the top picture have vanished.

The former Rhymney Railway Bridge in Adam Street.

The old bridge is no longer in existence and the wall has been replaced with the local magistrates court.

Cardiff ship engineer Joseph Robertson, who posed for this picture on his bicycle in the 1890s, opened a bicycle shop in Tudor Road. Born in 1866, he was lost at sea when his ship the HMS *Cumbria* sank without trace in 1899. And right: bicycles are still a popular mode of transport in Cardiff.

This 67-seater double entrance trolley bus was one of 15 supplied to Cardiff Corporation Transport Department by Bruce Coach Works Ltd, Cardiff. The last trolley bus ran in the city on 11 January 1970.

One of the modern-day buses in use in Cardiff today.

Cardiff Bridge, often mistakenly called Canton Bridge, was widened in 1931. The original medieval timbered bridge was replaced by a stone bridge in 1552. Several bridges built later could not withstand the storms and floods and the town bridge was rebuilt in 1859 and widened in 1877. The Marchioness of Bute opened the new widened bridge on 30 March 1931.

There may be more pedestrians in the previous picture than in this one. However, there is a remarkable lack of traffic in both photographs.

This fascinating picture was taken shortly after Duke Street was widened in 1924.

The clock is missing from the Fulton and Dunlop building but very little else has altered apart from the traffic and people.

This picture was taken before World War One and shows a proud taxi cab driver showing off his cab parked in Museum Place.

This taxi driver pictured outside Cardiff General Railway Station looks just as proud of his vehicle as the cab driver in the top photograph.

A motorised taxi cab is just one of the modes of transport that was seen in Queen Street at the turn of the century.

The clip clop of horses hooves and the rattle of the trams are no longer heard in the streets of Cardiff.

City Shops and Businesses

The entrance to the Central Market in St Mary Street can be seen in the centre of this photograph. The market was opened by the Lady Mayoress, the Marchioness of Bute, on 8 May 1891.

The original façade of the market was built in 1884, but was destroyed by a fire a year later. The present façade was built in 1886.

High Street was once the principal street of the medieval borough. The entrance to High Street Arcade is seen right of picture behind the vehicle parked outside the New Dorothy Café, *c.*1929.

High Street is much more busier these days at least traffic wise.

Stevens and Son Wine and Spirit Merchants, High Street, *c.*1874. In days of old, a twice weekly open air market was held in High Street every Wednesday and Saturday where local farmers would sell their produce.

The street has certainly changed for the better since the top picture was taken.

Anros Fashion Shop was situated at 7 High Street when this picture was taken in 1956. The entrance to the Mavis June School of Dancing was between Anros and Samuels right of picture. Note the Christmas tree above Samuels.

There has been little change to this building in the past 50 years.

Castle Arcade in High Street was built in 1887. A feature of the arcade is its first floor wooden gallery. Welsh Sports Limited was based there when this picture was taken in 1949.

Even the chimney stacks remain and little else has changed in more than a hundred years.

J. Gulliford & Sons the bookseller and stationers, 20 St Mary Street. The cars are parked in Wharton Street while the forecourt of the Sandringham Hotel can just about be seen on the extreme right. 1951.

The ornate windows remain and only the lower half of the building, which is now the Cheltenham and Gloucester Building Society, has been refurbished.

Littlewoods Stores, Queen Street. When this picture was taken in the late 1960s, the extension to Littlewoods in Charles Street was under construction. The extension was officially opened in 1970, but sadly the store closed in 1998.

Marks & Spencer have taken over from Littlewoods, but the *South Wales Echo* is still being sold from the same spot.

The Taff Vale public house right of picture had already been closed when this picture was taken around 1978. The Queen Street shoppers are seen walking past the quaintly named Paradise Place.

Hard to believe, looking at this picture, that in times long gone, Paradise Place had lived up to its name with its picturesque little suburban cottages and pretty front gardens.

Masters & Co Clothiers, Queen Street/Charles Street in 1914. The building dates to around 1869. There was a time when the local pack of hounds would meet near this spot.

The Burger King restaurant now occupies the corner. The building looks very much the same as it did more than a century ago.

Mill Lane open air market in the 1960s. The New Moon Club in New Street occupied the top floor of the wholesale clothing warehouse which overlooked the market.

Now the site of the Cardiff Marriot Hotel there is no sign of the open air market which had moved to there from The Hayes in 1953.

Castle Buildings, Womanby Street, *c.*1954. The name womanby is thought to mean 'the home or dwelling of the houndman or keeper of hounds.' In 1759, a fight took place in the street between the crew of the man-o-war Aldrough and the Eagle. The sailors were armed with pistols, swords, pikes and muskets. At the end of the bloody battle, one man lay dead and many were injured.

This part of Womanby Street has hardly changed in around 50 years.

The Norwich Union Insurance Society in Park Place is left of picture. The lady and gentleman walking into town are crossing over the feeder river.

The trees still stand but the railings over the feeder have vanished. Oakleigh House is left of picture.

On the right of picture is the Park Hall Buildings built in the French renaissance style and opened to the public in 1885. On the left can be seen S. Evans Lassam the ladies tailors c.1918.

The exterior of the Park Hotel, now part of the Thistle group, has hardly changed at all. The big difference, of course, is that Queen Street is now pedestrianised.

A lorry can be seen parked outside the popular Carlton Hotel restaurant in Queen Street. This picture was taken before the building was badly damaged by Nazi bombers in 1941.

Evan Roberts and the Carlton Hotel are long gone, but the Principality Building Society (note its dome in the background) is still helping Cardiffians to buy their own homes.

Seccombes & Co. had a store in Queen Street for many years and it was a sad day for many shoppers when it closed in 1977.

One wonders what the young men in the top picture would make of it all if they returned to the same spot today.

'The World's Greatest Bazaar' was situated at 5 St John's Street. To many Cardiffians, St John's Street is known as St John's Square.

The bay windows above the Delifrance café haven't changed that much and note that the ladder has been replaced by scaffolding!

Anderson & Co., who billed themselves as the 'Cheapest Clothiers in the World', eventually closed down to make way for the building of Morgan Arcade in St Mary Street, *c.*1890.

The windows over the Louis Restaurant left of picture tell us the exact location of where Anderson & Co. was situated.

The huge David Morgan stores on The Hayes is shown on the left of picture. In the centre can be seen the old central library which opened in 1882.

When this picture was taken the well-known David Morgan clock, left of top picture, was being repaired.

Leisure and Pleasure

The first purpose built theatre in Cardiff stood in Queen Street (Crockherbtown) and was opened in 1826. This picture shows Cardiffians enjoying a Punch and Judy show in The Hayes not far from where St David's Hall now stands, *c.*1890.

John Batchelor's statue was moved a few yards from its original place a few years ago. But crowds still flock to The Hayes to St David's Concert Hall officially opened by Queen Elizabeth, the Queen Mother in 1983.

The New Theatre on the corner of Park Place and Greyfriars Road was opened to the public in 1906 and over the years has provided all kinds of entertainment from pantomime to opera.

One wonders whether the tree left of picture can really be the same one as can be seen in the top picture.

The Pavilion Theatre in St Mary Street opened in 1877 as a variety theatre called the Philharmonic Hall. In 1892 it became Stoll's Panopticon until 1916 then reopened as the Pavilion Picture Theatre in 1918 until it closed in 1970.

The only reminder of its glorious past are the two pillars at the entrance.

Originally a roller skating rink, the Central Cinema on The Hayes opened as a cinema in 1911. It remained open as a cinema until 1958 and was later demolished.

Oxford Arcade now stands on the site of the Central Cinema.

The Prince of Wales on the corner of St Mary Street and Wood Street opened as the New Theatre Royal in 1878. It was completely gutted by a fire in 1899 and was entirely rebuilt. It became the Playhouse in 1920 and the Prince of Wales in 1935. Some of the great stage names that trod its boards included Laurence Olivier, John Gielgud, Richard Burton, Donald Wolfit, Rex Harrison and Margot Fonteyn.

The exterior of the building hasn't changed a lot, but the interior is now a restaurant and bar.

The much loved Capitol Cinema in Queen Street was opened in 1921 and provided the public with not only a cinema but a restaurant and a dance hall. It sadly closed in 1978.

This is the Capitol Exchange shopping complex which was built on the site of the Capitol Cinema.

The Gaumont in Queen Street was originally opened in 1887 as Levino's Hall. Two years later it was renamed the Empire Theatre then in 1954 it became the Gaumont until it closed in 1961.

This picture was taken just before C & A closed down in January 2001.

The Queen's Cinema at 92 Queen Street was opened in 1909 as the Cardiff Cinema Theatre. The first cinema in Cardiff to show a 'talkie', Al Jolson's *The Singing Fool*, it closed in 1955 after the screening of *African Queen*.

To the left of picture can be seen part of the National Westminster Bank. Fifty years ago the Queen's Cinema was transporting Cardiffians to exotic places around the world albeit in mind rather than body. Now Going Places has taken over the role.

The Park Hall Cinema in Park Place opened as a concert hall in 1885 and became a cinema in 1916. It closed in 1971.

Thirty-one years later and the Park Hall Cinema is now a bar. The Park Hotel right of picture is now known as the Thistle Hotel.

The Sophia Gardens Pavilion, built for the Festival of Britain, was opened in 1951 but closed down 30 years later in 1981 when the roof caved in after a heavy snowstorm. Some people will remember the wrestling and boxing tournaments that took place there while others will recall the Saturday dances. Cliff Richards and Danny Kaye were just two of the big stars to appear there.

Sophia Gardens bowling club now stands in Sophia Gardens but not on the exact spot as the old pavilion.

The Wales Empire Pool shortly before it was demolished to make way for the Millennium Stadium. It was built by Cardiff Corporation for the 1958 Empire and Commonwealth Games and to provide Cardiffians with a modern swimming pool.

Many Cardiffians have deplored the fact that these new buildings obscure the new magnificent Millennium Stadium and it is not hard to see why.

For more than a century, the old free library in Trinity Street served the citizens of the town well. The Free Library extension was opened by the Prince of Wales, later King Edward VII, in 1896. The new Cardiff and County Council Library in Frederick Street was opened in 1987.

The Pallas Athene on the southern façade of the library is now obscured by the trees which have grown since the top picture was taken and the statue of John Batchelor has been moved a few yards forward.

The Royal Oak Inn which was situated at 59 St Mary Street is said to date to 1683. To the right of picture is The Blue Anchor, *c.*1882.

La Brasserie Restaurant now stands on the site of the Royal Oak Inn.

On the west side of St Mary Street is the Royal Hotel which was opened in 1866. Horse and carriages were the main source of transport when this picture was taken not that long after it was built.

The Royal Hotel was undergoing a multi-million pound refurbishment when this picture was taken in May 2001.

The Borough Arms in St Mary Street was established around 1873. It has also been known from time to time as The Bodega, *c.*1891.

Since the picture on the previous page was taken the Borough Arms has been entirely rebuilt but the buildings either side of it are easily recognisable.

Originally called the Steam Mill Arms, the Terminus right of picture, was renamed The Terminus in 1882.

The Terminus is now known as Sam's Bar and is said to be haunted. Surprisingly there wasn't much traffic about when this picture was taken.

The Mason's Arms was situated in Queen Street (earlier Smith Street) from 1795 until 1920. The postbox left of picture, behind the gentleman wearing a bowler, is believed to have been the first one in Cardiff.

The Mason's Arms was situated near the entrance of what is now Superdrug.

The Taff Vale Inn, on the corner of Paradise Place and Queen Street, had stood on the same spot for nearly a hundred years until it was demolished in 1978. It had already closed down when this picture was taken.

Queen Street remains just as busy today as it was when the top picture was taken more than 300 years ago.

The Red Lion stood on the corner of Kingsway and Queen Street (formerly North Street and Smith Street) between 1792 and 1958.

Lloyds TSB and Pizza Hut now stand on the site of the Red Lion.

The British Volunteer Hotel on The Hayes dated to 1882. It was popular for the hot dinners it served *c.*1890.

Another part of central Cardiff which has been transformed over the years.

The fifth Marquis of Bute gave Cardiff Castle and Bute Park to Cardiff in 1947.

This picture was taken in winter time and trees now obscure the west view of Cardiff Castle and Bute Park.

The Three Horse Shoes stood at number 22 High Street between 1798 and 1913.

The Bradford and Bingley Building Society had closed its High Street branch when this picture was taken in March 2001.

North-west view of Cardiff Castle
and the outer moat.

The bridge in the opposite picture was built in 1879. It was dismantled in 1927 and moved to another part of the castle grounds and was demolished in 1963.

Gorsedd Gardens in Cathays Park was opened to the public in July 1910. The statue depicts Lord Ninian Crichton Stuart who was killed in action during World War One.

The statue hasn't been removed. It's just that the photographer couldn't take this picture at the exact spot as the top one was taken without standing in the middle of a flower bed!

A Vanished Docklands

The impressive Pierhead Building, designed in French Gothic style, was built in 1896 and housed the offices of the Bute Dock Company. A Grade I listed building, from 1923 until 1947 it was the headquarters of the Great Western Railway. It later became the administrative office of the Port of Cardiff, *c.*1903.

Roath Basin, Bute Docks, at the turn of the century. The sailing ship extreme right is the *Antonio*.

The Queen Alexandra Dock was opened on 13 July 1907 by King Edward VII and Queen Alexandra.

For the smooth handling of all types of cargo – from coal to oranges – the docks were well equipped.

Clarence Road Bridge was opened by the Duke of Clarence in 1890.

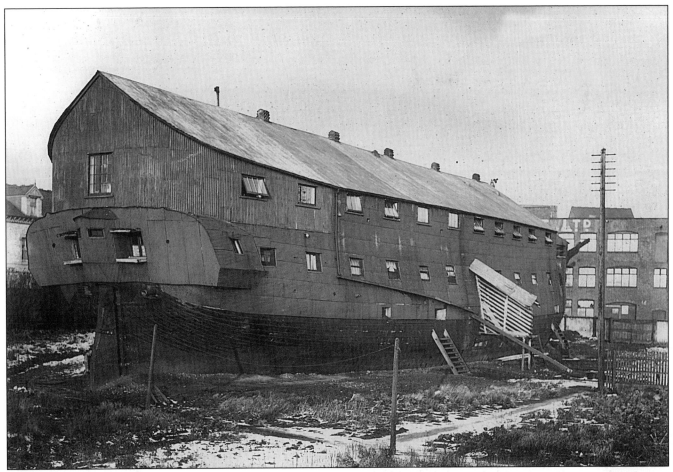

In 1860, the HMS *Havannah* sailed into the East Bute Dock. It was later berthed near Penarth Road Bridge and was converted to an industrial school for boys.

For more than a hundred years pleasure steamers have been operating in the Bristol Channel.

In 1910, Captain R.F.C. Scott's ship *Terra Nova* sailed from Cardiff Docks for the South Pole. This postcard was originally printed by E. Davies & Co of Paradise Place, Cardiff, on the return of the ship in 1913. The postcard was reprinted and presented to The Captain Scott Society by A. McLay & Co Ltd of Cardiff.

Not the *Terra Nova*, but the *Sir Winston Churchill* training ship on a visit to Cardiff in the 1970s.

General scene of the dock.

Timber imports to Cardiff came from Scandinavia, Russia and Newfoundland. This picture shows timber vessels berthed at Fletcher's Wharf in Roath Dock.

The discharging of timber at Fletcher's Wharf, Roath Dock, using mechanical handling appliances.

Dockers discharging boxes of oranges direct to road vehicles.

Dockers handling the pallets of fruit in sheds at the docks.

Frozen meat being
unloaded at Kings
Wharf.

British Road Services vehicles being loaded with boxes of butter and zinc ingots at the Queen Alexandra Docks.

The mobile coal hoists were capable of dealing speedily with 20-ton wagons.

Dock workers loading cars at the Queen Alexandra Dock.

Guest Keen and Nettlefolds (South Wales Limited) Rolling Mill, Tremorfa. The company had the most efficient bar and hot strip mill, wire rod mill and nail factory in Europe. Sadly, the factory closed in 1978.

These machines were capable of producing 800 tons of nails per week.

John Meazey took this picture in the early 1970s, which shows Cardiff Docklands in the background, from the 10th floor of the Julian Hodge building in Newport Road.

The Norwegian Seaman Mission Church, east side of the West Bute Dock, 1967.

When this picture was taken in 1906, Nellie Collins was the landlady of the Albion Hotel in Bute Street.

The Custom House in Bute Street was dated to 1859 and was demolished in 1998.

The famed Windsor Hotel was popularly known as The Big Windsor to distinguish it from the nearby smaller Windsor Arms. First licenced in 1855, it served the best food in Cardiff and many well-known personalities visited there including Katharine Hepburn and Noel Coward.

The Cornish Mount, Patrick Street, Butetown, was shortly demolished after this picture was taken in 1967.

The White Hart Inn, James Street, Butetown. Sidney Peel was mine host when this picture was taken around 1898. Mr Peel's daughter, Mary, was born in the inn on 10 June 1879. As Mrs Mary Lewis she later lived at 'Staincliffe', Philog Road, Whitchurch, Cardiff.

Cardiff Bay Today

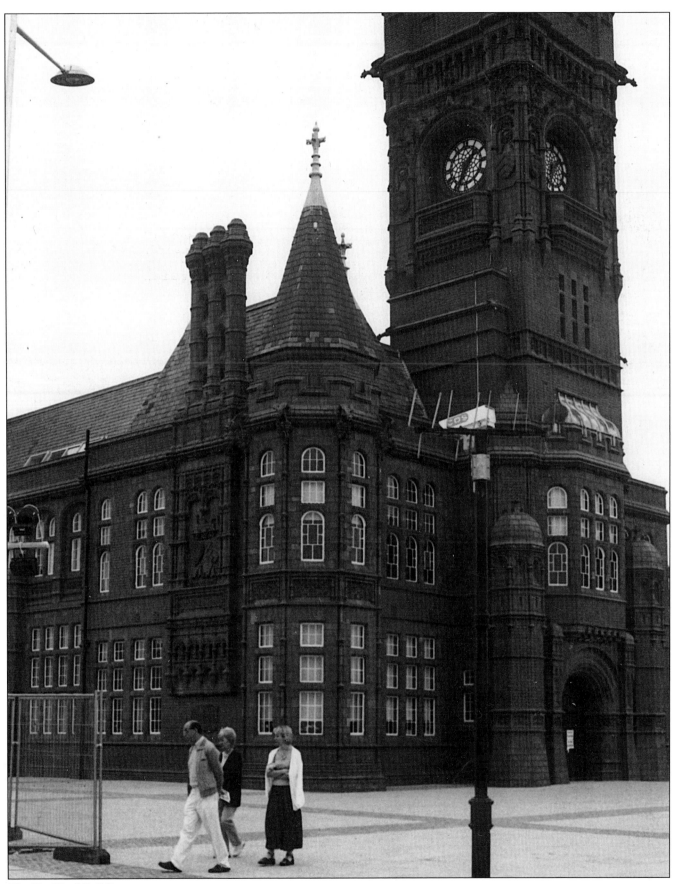

The Pier Head Building.

The reflection of the Pier Head Building can be seen in the inner harbour sea water.

The historic Pilotage House. Pilots based here safely brought in ships through the narrow entrance channels thus avoiding collisions with other vessels. The building now houses Woods Brasserie. To the right of picture is the Windsor Hotel.

Lock-keeper's House. From this little building, the lock-keeper controlled the entrance to the Roath Basin. It is now used as a coffee shop.

The present-day Norwegian Church Arts Centre is a replica of the church which served Norwegian seamen from 1866 to 1959 and which was originally located on the eastern side of the West Bute Dock.

St David's Hotel and Spa.

When the planned fresh water Barrage is finished the public will be able to walk between Penarth (right of picture) and Queen Alexandra Harbour. The water front development will have picnic areas, landscaped gardens and cycling paths, creating a promenade.

Mermaid Quay. A number of open air concerts – from pop to opera – have already been performed in Cardiff Bay.

Techniquest, the family hands-on science centre left of picture, is situated on the site of the old Sailor's Home in Stuart Street which was built in 1855 to provide seamen with cheap board and lodging.

It is hard to believe looking at this picture that Cardiff Docks was once the premier port in the United Kingdom. The deserted office buildings of C.H. Bailey Ltd can be seen in the background.

Located in the Roath Basin is the *Helwick* LV14. This 550 tons lightship with an overall length of 137 feet, was situated on the Gower Peninsula. The beam from its light tower could be seen from 25 miles and warned ships of the Helwick Swatch, a treacherous sand bank.

Around and About

Beulah Road, Rhiwbina. Beaulah Congregational Church left of picture still survives which is more than can be said for the china and glass store adjacent to it, *c*.1958.

The wall in front of the church in the top picture has gone but apart from the motor vehicles very little else has changed.

Llanishen village was much more peaceful in the 1950s when this postcard picture was taken.

The street lighting is different and trees and hedges now obscure some of the houses.

Newport Road. The building on the right is St James's Church which was consecrated in 1894. On the left can be seen the Wesleyan Methodist Church demolished in 1955, *c*.1903.

To the left of this picture can be seen the steeple of Clifton Street Welsh Calvinist Methodist Church.

The Royal Infirmary, Newport Road, was built at a cost of £23,000 in 1883. Once known as the King Edward VII Hospital, it was closed in 1998. The chapel left of picture was added in 1921.

The tram lines and overhead cables are long gone and just one tree remains.

The Cardiff Power Station in Colchester Avenue. It was built in 1902 and closed in 1970.

The pre-war cooling towers were demolished in 1972. Railings have replaced part of the wall but the street lighting remains the same.

This single storey warehouse in Newport Road had recently been constructed when Stephenson & Alexander had it up for sale in 1959.

Courts Furnishing Stores, which used to be in High Street in the city centre, now stands on the site.

A Brownhills Garages, Herbert Street, just off North Road and almost opposite Maindy Stadium, *c*.1950.

The houses, right of top picture, have vanished, but the garage building can still be seen.

When it opened in 1951, Maindy Stadium was dubbed the Welsh White City.

The cycle track remains, but the running track and grandstand has gone. The top of the Pearl Assurance building can be seen in the background.

In 1933 Western Avenue bridge was opened to traffic but there's no sign of a vehicle in this picture.

Behind the bridge left of picture can be seen some of the houses on the vast Gabalfa housing estate which sprang up in the 1950s.

St Martin's Church, Albany Road was formally opened on 14 September 1901. Albany Road used to be known as Merthyr Road but was renamed after the Duke of Albany died. The exterior of the church was bombed during the blitz and was restored in 1955.

The house left of the top picture is now the Indiana Balti House Restaurant and Parsons Motor Services is now the Consul Suncenter.

There were no parking problems in Carlisle Street, Splott, when this picture was taken in Victorian times.

Carlisle Street and Ordell Street have certainly changed since the top picture was taken and some would say not for the better.

The Corporation Hotel on the corner of Cowbridge Road East and Llandaff Road, 1908.

The Corporation Hotel has recently been refurbished to make it more appealing to the younger generation.

The Royal George Hotel on the corner of Crwys Road and Mackintosh Place in 1924.

Traffic wise, Crwys Road and Mackintosh Place are a lot busier these days. The pub was known as Clancy's Irish Bar for a few years, but is now called The George.

ALFRED LOUGHER & SON. LTD.

156 **LOUGHER'S** 156

REFRIGERATED WINDOW

LOUGHER

Alfred Lougher & Son Ltd. The popular butchers in Cowbridge Road East, 1964.

Next page: The top part of the building has changed very little. Johnsons the dry cleaners and Klick Photopoint are situated where the butcher's shop once stood.

Pope's Photo Service and
Library, Cowbridge Road
East, 1934.

Dennis Pope's photo services business established in 1925 is still holding out against strong opposition.

The Penylan Cinema on the corner of Wellfield Road and Albany Road in 1926. Later renamed the Globe Cinema, it was demolished shortly after it closed in 1985.

One would hardly recognise the spot from the above picture today.

An animated Clifton Street in 1909.

If it wasn't for the spire of Clifton Street Welsh Calvinistic Methodist Chapel one would hardly think these two pictures were of the same street.

The demolition of Crwys Road School in August 1973. Lloyds Bank can be seen on the left of the picture.

The Pioneer Co-Operative Supermarket now stands on the site of Crwys Road School which was attended by Frederick Barter who won the Victoria Cross during World War One.

The Blue Bell Inn, St Mellons, before World War Two.

The Blue Bell Inn and The White Hart left of picture have both seen many changes over the years as these two pictures illustrate. The clue is the long chimney pot left of building.

Generations of Cardiffians have enjoyed walking along the promenade in Roath Park which was opened to the public on 20 June 1894, pictured *c*.1953.

The well-known lighthouse-clock tower memorial to Captain Robert Falcon Scott and his companions had just been repainted when this picture was taken.

Roath Park Lake in Edwardian times. The lighthouse-clock tower had not been built when this postcard picture was taken.

The lighthouse-clock tower can be seen in the distance in this photograph. The railings appear to be the same ones as in the top picture.